Hearing

Claire Llewellyn

W
FRANKLIN WATTS
LONDON • SYDNEY

First published in 2005 by Franklin Watts
338 Euston Road, London, NW1 3BH

Franklin Watts Australia
Level 17/207 Kent Street, Sydney NSW 2000

Text copyright © Claire Llewellyn 2004
Design and concept © Franklin Watts 2004

Series advisers: Gill Matthews, non-fiction literacy
    consultant and Inset trainer
Editor: Rachel Cooke
Series design: Peter Scoulding
Designer: James Marks
Photography: Ray Moller unless otherwise credited
Acknowledgements: Mike Allwood-Coppin/Eye Ubiquitous: 4bl.
J. Heras/Still Pictures: 15tr. Philip Marazzi/Ecoscene: 13t.
James Marchington/Ecoscene: 21. B. Odeur/Still Pictures: 7tr.
Joseph Okwesa/Trip: 4cr. H. Rogers/Trip: 15tl. Paul Seheult/Eye Ubiquitous: 18.
Jorgen Shytte/Still Pictures: 20t. Eric Smith/Trip: 17bl. Paul A. Souders/Corbis: 11tr.
Thanks to our models, including Vanessa Dang, Sophie Hall, Latifah Harris, Thomas Howe, Amelia
Menicou, Spencer Mulchay and Ishar Sehgal.

ISBN: 978 0 7496 8895 0

Printed in Malaysia

Franklin Watts is a division of Hachette Children's Books, an Hachette UK company.
www.hachettelivre.co.uk

Contents

We hear with our ears

We use our ears to hear sounds in the world around us. Hearing is one of our senses.

▽ *Our ears hear a plane in the sky...*

the workmen in the road...

a friend calling…

a clock ticking…

We have five senses. They are seeing, hearing, tasting, smelling and touching.

our tummy rumbling.

Looking at ears

We have two ears, one on each side of our head. We hear when a sound goes into our ears.

▶ *Look at a friend's ear. You can't see all of it. Part of it is hidden inside the head.*

Try covering one ear with your hand, then the other. What happens to the sounds you hear?

The shape of the ear helps us to hear well.

The bat's big ears help it to hear well so it can hunt for insects in the dark.

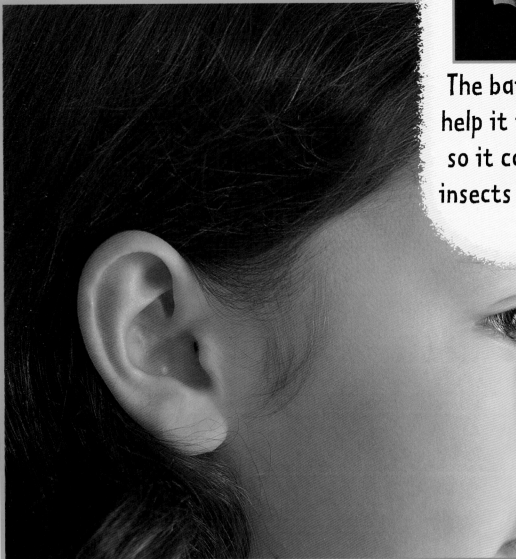

All sorts of sounds

Our ears hear all sorts of sounds. We can tell one sound from another.

We can tell if a sound is soft...

or loud.

We can tell if a sound is high...

Stand in a circle of friends and ask them to take turns making a sound. Say if each sound is loud or soft and high or low.

or low.

9

Hearing voices

We hear people speaking every day. We know many people by the sound of their voice.

Dad has a low voice.

Mum has a high voice.

Ask three friends to stand behind you and take turns saying something. Who is speaking each time?

Gran has a soft voice.

My brother has a loud voice.

Follow the sound

Our ears help us to tell where a sound is coming from. They tell us if it is near or far away.

► *Miaow! I can hear my cat. But where is he?*

Miaow! The cat sounds louder now… He must be near.

Lions live in a group. Sometimes one of the group loses the others and roars loudly. The other lions roar back so the lost lion can find them.

Miaow! There he is – up the stairs!

13

Keeping safe

Our hearing helps to keep us safe. It warns us of danger.

▶ *A smoke alarm bleeps very loudly. It warns us there is a fire.*

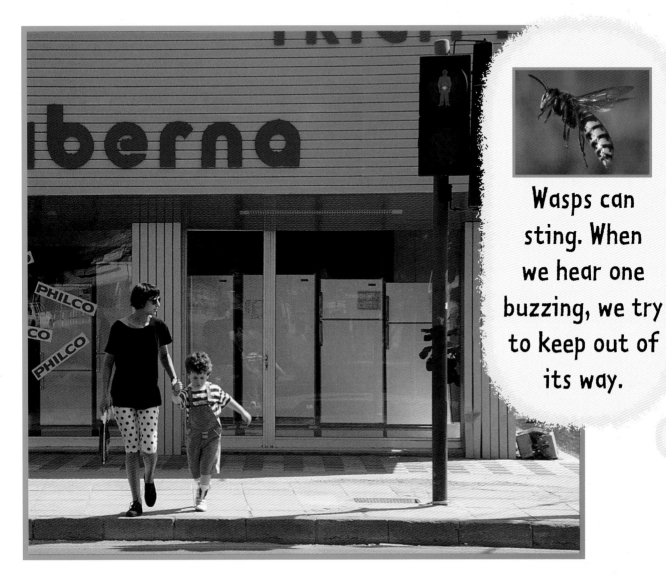

Wasps can sting. When we hear one buzzing, we try to keep out of its way.

We don't just look when we cross the road. We listen as well.

Keeping in touch

Our hearing helps us to talk and listen. It helps us to keep in touch.

▶ *We learn to talk by hearing other people speak.*

16

We listen when we are face to face…

or on the phone.

Some parrots can talk. They learn to do this by listening to people and copying what they say.

Some people cannot hear

Deaf people cannot hear well. They cannot hear what people are saying.

▶ *Some people wear a hearing aid.*

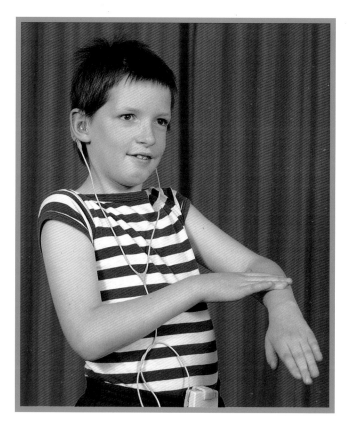

Hearing aids work by making everything sound louder.

Others learn to read hand signs...

or people's lips.

Looking after our ears

Our ears are very important.
We must look after them.

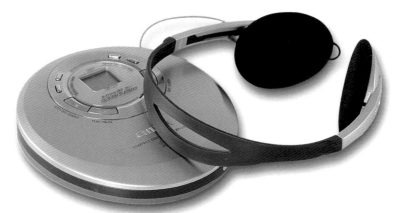

Never put small things inside your ears.

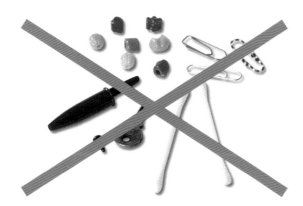

Don't play music too loud. Loud sounds can hurt our ears.

People who do noisy jobs wear ear muffs to protect their ears.

Our ears make a sticky wax. The wax protects and cleans our ears. It also traps tiny bits of dirt and dust.

I know that...

1 We use our ears to hear.

2 Hearing is one of our senses.

3 We have two ears. Their shape helps us to hear well.

4 We can tell if a sound is high or low, loud or soft.

5 We know many people by the sound of their voice.

6 We can hear where a sound is coming from.

7 Our hearing helps to keep us safe.

8 Hearing helps us to talk and listen.

9 Some people cannot hear.

10 We must look after our ears.

Index

deaf 18
ear 4, 6, 7, 8, 12,
    20, 21, 22
far 12
hearing aid 18
high 9, 10, 22

listen 15, 16,
    17, 23
loud 8, 9, 11, 13,
    14, 18, 20, 22
low 9, 10, 22
near 12, 13

sense 4, 5, 22
soft 8, 9, 11, 22
sound 4, 6, 8, 9,
    10, 12, 18, 23
speak 10, 11, 16
talk 16, 17, 23

About this book

I Know That! is designed to introduce children to the process of gathering information and using reference books, one of the key skills needed to begin more formal learning at school. For this reason, each book's structure reflects the information books children will use later in their learning career – with key information in the main text and additional facts and ideas in the captions. The panels give an opportunity for further activities, ideas or discussions. The contents page and index are helpful reference guides.

The language is carefully chosen to be accessible to children just beginning to read. Illustrations support the text but also give information in their own right; active consideration and discussion of images is another key referencing skill. The main aim of the series is to build confidence – showing children how much they already know and giving them the ability to gather new information for themselves. With this in mind, the I know that... section at the end of the book is a simple way for children to revisit what they already know as well as what they have learnt from reading the book.